Feminism in Urdu Literature

Compiled By:
Mukarram Niyaz

© Taemeer Publications
Feminism in Urdu Literature
by: Mukarram Niyaz

Edition: March '2025

Publisher:

Taemeer Publications LLC (Michigan, USA / Hyderabad, India)

© **Taemeer Publications**
[Each Article rights reserved with its respective Author]

Book	:	Feminism in Urdu Literature
Author	:	Mukarram Niyaz
Publisher	:	Taemeer Publications
Year	:	'2025
Pages	:	94
Title Design	:	*Taemeer Web Design*

CONTENTS

Ismat Chughtai... Iconic Feminist Writer
                                Ashraf Lone   4

Women's World Of Urdu Writing
                                  Pragya Roy   10

A woman writer's words can spark transformation
                                  JS Ifthekhar   17

Rashid Jahan: The Bad Girl Of Urdu Literature
                                Vaishnavi Mahurkar   22

Feminism in Urdu Literature
                                  Lalit Gupta   29

Feminism and Rashid-ul-Khairi
                                  Rauf Parekh   34

The 'F' factor in Urdu Literature
                                  Shazia Tasneem   39

Translating 'Feminism' in Urdu
                                  Sheema Kermani   48

Fahmida Riaz's fearless legacy
                                  Aleezeh Fatima   57

The future is feminist literature
                                  Khadija Muzaffar   68

Fahmida Riaz: The act of translation as mourning
                                  Asad Alvi   80

Sahir Ludhianvi's Ode To Women
                                  Raza Naeem   88

Ismat Chughtai: The Iconic Feminist Writer Of Urdu Literature
Ashraf Lone

Ismat Chughtai (1915-1991) born in a small town in Badayun, Uttar Pradesh is one of the best short story writers, and one among the first few feminist writers in Urdu literature. Ismat Chughtai is considered a trend setter in Urdu short stories and she touched upon new topics which were considered taboo when Urdu literature was in its infancy, and its scope of topics was very limited. Ismat wrote eloquently on the issues of women of lower and lower middle class.

Ismat knew about the issues and problems of women of her era and took keen interest in highlighting these through her short stories. She laments about the wretchedness and plight of women and of being uneducated. She wants to see women free from any male bondage and suppression.

"Chauthi Ka Joda" (The Wedding Suit) is about a poor widow, Bi Amma who has two daughters, Kubra and Hameeda. The story focuses on Bi Amma's obsession to get Kubra married as soon as possible, but every time she nears her goal of marrying off Kubra, something terrible happens and Kubra's marriage remains on hold. And then one day Kubra's and Hameeda's cousin Rahat arrives at their home for a stay for one month for police training. Hameeda, sister of Kubra feels happy on this and tells Bi Amma to use this opportunity to impress Rahat to marry Kubra. They leave no stone unturned to make Rahat's stay comfortable at their home and leave everything at his disposal. But Rahat develops interest in Hameeda and flirts with her by making livid remarks and touches her inappropriately on various occasions and after a month Rahat leaves without marrying any one of them and this leaves Bi Amma devasted. Bi Amma laments on the fate of Kubra,

"Khuda ne soorat nahin di, isi liye rahat uski taraf dekhta tak nahin" (Rahat doesn't even look at her because God hasn't given her fair features).

This shows how society, especially the lower class is worried about the complexion of the girl and how it is one of the obstacles in getting a girl married. On leaving Rahat, Kubra dies the next morning of TB and thus comes an unexpected end to a miserable and wretched life of a poor girl. And, "Chauthi Ka Joda" becomes Kubra's shroud. The story depicts how financial burden is another reason for the plight of a lower and lower middle class women. Rahat's character shows how men in privileged positions easily get away with their wrongdoings.

In "Jadein" (Roots) Ismat tells a story about an old woman who is unable to understand the intricacies of Partition. She doesn't want to leave her house for newly formed Pakistan. She loves her roots and doesn't want to get cutoff from her roots. She is not ready to leave her land, country and her neighbors and likens this leaving to death.

"Time passed on, but Amma stayed steadfast in her position like a banyan tree that stands upright through storms and blizzards."

"You all go. As for me, where shall I go at this age." Amma tells Sardar Ali, the leader of the National Guards. Finally, Amma's sons, daughters, son-in-laws, daughter-in-laws and other relatives start to leave the house for newly formed Pakistan, Amma's heart flutters and tears come in her eyes and she thinks:

"Who knows whether the new soil will be conducive to these saplings or make them wilt. These poor saplings."

Amma couldn't sleep the whole night, thinking whether his sons and daughter and other relatives will be able to survive or get killed in the way. And after sometime her Hindu neighbor Roopchandji brings back her children from Loni railway station and Amma heaves a sigh of relief. Thus, a happy family is saved from this devastating partition which destroyed lacs of lives dividing thousands of families. The story also depicts love between Hindus and Muslims not ready for partition.

"Lihaaf" (Quilt) is a story about homosexuality. It is a story about a women namely Begum Jaan, who doesn't get the required attention and sexual satisfaction from her husband Nawab and this neglect ruins her life. The husband of Begum Jaan, Nawab takes much interest in young and fair boys. Begum Jaan feels dejected and frustrated with this neglect of Nawab and then, it was Rabbu who rescued her from the fall. Soon her thin body began to fill out. Her cheeks began to glow and she blossomed in beauty. It was a special oil massage that brought life back to the half-dead Begum Jaan. Sorry, you won't find the recipe for this oil even in the most exclusive magazines.

And we see how Begum Jaan's life and eventually a family is ruined and destroyed, as Begum Jaan falls to lesbianism.

"Kaisi Biwi Kaisa Shohar"(Husband and Wife) is a story of woman named Aamina whose husband initially loves her very much, but after sometime loses interest in her and Aamina becomes:

"The severely beaten living woman in the world."

Aamina also faces harsh treatment from her mother-in-law and initially ignores everything, but when after sometime she sees no improvement in the behavior of her husband and mother-in-law, she protests and revolts against this oppression and exploitation.

Aamina starts giving tuition to children and helps her husband and thus shows the way to other woman who are suppressed from centuries to raise their voice against the injustices meted out to them. And through Aamina's character, Ismat wants to depict a woman who is independent and free from oppression and exploitation.

Also read: Celebrating The 107th Birth Anniversary Of Ismat Chughtai: A Stalwart Of Feminist Movement

Ismat Chughtai, in her short stories has depicted the oppression and misery of middle class Muslim women with artistic depth. She knows the language of these women and her characters speak this language with finesse and ease and with much boldness, and here lies the distinctness and greatness of Ismat Chughtai.

Ref.: youthkiawaaz.com

***

Women's World Of Urdu Writing : In Conversation With Smriti Bhoker

Pragya Roy

Smriti Bhoker is an Urdu poet who is currently pursuing a masters degree in sociology from Delhi. Urdu, as Smriti herself calls, is a "dying language". Besides the annual visits to Rekhta fests, I too have massively failed to engage with Urdu's world of expressions—be it sadness, happiness, love or resistance—and its varied forms like poetry, ghazals, shayari or stories. However, despite our collective ignorance of the language's power and poise, we still manage to learn a few of its words; thanks to Bollywood and its fetishising tendencies.

However, for people like Smriti, who do not simply learn, speak, read or write in Urdu, but also express and live through the language, the approach is not limited to song lyrics or dialogues from pop-culture. For them, the horizon is ever expanding, where they themselves are a very crucial part of its evolution.

Her Urdu satires reflect the current

deplorable socio-political scenario of the country—the religious hatred, the patriarchal society and the obscurity of freedom—all packed together in her pieces. They give you a reality check—one that you are already, sub-consciously aware of, but you fail to ponder over in your everyday. These stories are narrated with a distinct style of oration, which make them even more appealing.

In conversation with Smriti Bhoker, about her journey with the Urdu language, and its future.

The love ran out, and thankfully satire doesn't need a lot of love. Satire needs unadulterated bitterness and that's an equally motivating drive.

When and why did you start reading and writing in Urdu?

Smriti Bhoker: I used to write English poetry in school and I was beginning to take it seriously in my second year of graduation when my father suggested me to translate some of my work for him. According to him, since my upbringing was done in a house where 4-5 languages were spoken, he felt my hold of Urdu and Hindi would naturally be better than English and he was right! Both my parents were avid reader of Urdu literature and Panjabi folk, qawwali and ghazals were my household's background music. For the longest time, I have tried to run away from my own languages. When I developed an interest in Urdu literature, my dad told me about a few poems he wrote when he was young, one of them about my mother when he was away for training. My father who is now in the army, tells me that he wanted to be a poet when he was young; he just didn't have the luxury of a family that would support him on it, or the money to afford the life of a writer. As a result of this, the support for my work at home has been radical.

Who or what inspired you to indulge in this field of Urdu satires? What are the ways through which the gender question appear in your writing as well as in the domain of Urdu satires?

Smriti Bhoker: Poetry needs a ridiculous amount of love. For about two years, I only wrote poetry. While doing that, I had started to educate myself on social issues as I was following the lead of Faiz, Jalib and Paash. The love that is foundational for any kind of poetry to come forth died, the reason being the current times we are living in. Even my book that comes out this year, which is a collection of resistance poetry, has very few ghazals that were written post 2017. The love ran out, and thankfully satire doesn't need a lot of love. Satire needs unadulterated bitterness and that's an equally motivating drive.

My answer for the second part of the question is that I was a feminist before I started writing. So naturally one of the questions that one would ask while indulging in Urdu literature is that why doesn't it have enough women writers? The ones it does have either come from extremely privileged backgrounds or extremely disturbed ones. I saw my poetry was still accepted to some extent but my politics is where I saw a lot eyes rolling. This is something you would notice in the prestigious Urdu literature circles as well—my satires usually cover gender-politics not because it interests me or because it agitates my conservative relatives (I mean those reasons are tempting enough) but I primarily cover them because here isn't enough material on it in the form of satire by women.

My satires usually cover gender-politics not because it interests me or because it agitates my conservative relatives (I mean those reasons are tempting enough) but I primarily cover them because here isn't enough material on it in the form of satire by women.

Do you see yourself continue in this field, in future? Do you plan to translate it into a more professional field of interest?

SB: I'm hoping to continue in this field, not just as a satirist and a poet but eventually a playwright and scriptwriter too. I plan to write on Urdu and Punjabi literature academically as well. For now, I would like to read more and learn Bengali.

The oration of your satires demand a certain set of skills. Where did you learn them and what can you tell us about its importance in presentation of satires?

SB: There is a brilliant voice artist by the name of Fawad Khan who covers Manto's essays and Chugati's stories. He makes Manto's work sound better than any voice artist I have ever heard and I have heard him recite a lot of Manto. It's interesting that there is not much about him that I know except that he used to live in Pakistan. Yet everything I know about oration comes from him or from Zia Mohiuddin's collected recitals. I do this exercise where I hear what my satire would sound like if Fawad Khan had read them. Then I read them like Zia Mohiuddin would. After these two exercises, I read them as Smriti would read them.

Since a lot of people do not prefer reading anymore it's good to know how to present your work. However, I still believe we should try to go for authentic writers as opposed to those who know how to orate their work effectively.

If there is someone reading this now and wants to get involved in this field, what all suggestions do you want to give them?

SM: READ, read Urdu as much as you can. It's a dying language and what's left of it was claimed by Karan Johar's idea of Saba who is the pop culture reference for what Urdu women writers should look like. Pop culture also makes this language look like an accessory for the urban elite when it's historically one of the greatest weapon used against them. Make sure your foundation comes from the Urdu that used to inspire and provoke thought.

Lastly, tell us about your bitter-sweet journey with this field.

SM: There is a dilemma that I have lived in, ever since I started out. I have been as hopeful as the promise of a better tomorrow in the eyes of a drunk student who has just discovered Faiz Ahmed Faiz's resistance poetry and as hopeless as the drunk professor's faith in the system who has to teach this poetry in the morning. My journey is me in the place of the student some nights, and some nights the professor. Since election, sometimes it's both. I started out as a fangirl of Gulzar thinking Urdu starts and ends at Khushboo and now I cannot conceive a form of revolution that isn't the embodiment of this language. With that I am also ready to write a satire on why this imagined revolution will fail.

Ref.: feminisminindia.com

***

A woman writer's words can spark transformation
JS Ifthekhar

When a woman rises, she lifts not only herself but all women around her—and when that woman is a writer, her words can spark transformation. The two-day Bainul Aqwami Nisai Adabi Tanzeem (BANAT) conference which concluded at the Urdu Hall here on Thursday (October 31, 2024) drew around 70 women Urdu writers from 18 states.

The conference which marked the 8th Foundation Day of BANAT provided a unique forum for exchanging ideas and inspiring one another. This is for the first time that so many women writers gathered under one roof, a testament to their resilience, strength, and progress. The conference brought together voices from across the spectrum of women's Urdu literature. Discussions centered on the social, cultural, and gendered landscapes shaping the 21st century, highlighting the need for women to boldly voice their experiences and perspectives.

These writers are more than just storytellers; they are trailblazers who have shattered glass ceilings, questioned societal norms, and cleared paths for future generations. Through their prose and poetry, they have woven narratives of empowerment, determination, and courage. The energy in the gathering was undeniable—a collective of powerful voices, each one committed to illuminating the unique challenges and triumphs of women in today's world. As many as nine books written by women writers were released on the occasion by Prof. S.A. Shukoor, Director of Dairatul Maarif.

BANAT is 7-year-old

BANAT began modestly in October 2017, when a handful of women writers united through a WhatsApp group to share stories and exchange ideas. This simple yet powerful platform laid the foundation for what would become a dynamic collective, fostering creativity and collaboration. "Through this platform, we discussed stories and exchanged ideas," shared BANAT President Dr. Nigar Azeem, highlighting how this grassroots effort evolved into a national network of Urdu women writers advocating for cultural preservation and freedom of expression.

She emphasized the importance of women sharing their narratives authentically, making them a guiding light for future generations. Women's literature should reflect strength and autonomy, she said, and urged female writers not to censor their viewpoints or suppress their creative spirit. This assertiveness is not only essential for the growth of Urdu literature but also crucial in ensuring women stand as equals in both literary and social spheres.

Vow to honour Banu's legacy

Titled aptly as *Banu Ke Shahar Main BANAT*, the conference honored the legacy of Padma Shri awardee Jeelani Banu, one of Urdu's most celebrated fiction writers. Jeelani Banu's work has long illuminated the complexities of women's lives, inspiring generations to write with courage and conviction. The conference paid homage to her contributions, while also urging today's writers to keep her spirit alive by boldly expressing their truths.

Prof. Ameena Tahseen, conference convener and Head, Department of Women Education, MANUU, recalled how earlier there were a few women writers who sat behind curtains during programmes. Today they were on the stage, portraying the realities of struggle and resilience, and holding a mirror to society's injustices.

Make your voices heard

In an age where stories can serve as catalysts for change, BANAT encouraged its members to make their voices heard, undeterred by any attempts to silence them, said Azra Naqvi, vice president, BANAT.

A key concern addressed during the conference was the need to safeguard the Urdu script, 'rasm-ul-khat. BANAT's President, Tasneem Kausar, Secretary, BANAT emphasized this issue, warning of the dangers posed by its gradual erosion. "We have to protect it at all costs," she asserted, urging writers to preserve this cultural heritage. The conference served as a powerful reminder that these writers are not only the custodians of language but also champions of social change, weaving narratives that capture the challenges and aspirations of their time.

As feminist Urdu literature evolves, it carries the power to challenge stereotypes, confront societal norms, and inspire transformation. BANAT's conference underscored that the written word is a potent tool for shaping discourse and empowering women, reaffirming the belief that women must continue to leave their indelible mark in literature and beyond.

Feminism in Urdu

Urdu feminist literature has a rich history, shaped by women writers who have fearlessly voiced social and personal themes. Pioneers like Ismat Chughtai, Quratulain Hyder, and Jeelani Bano paved the way, addressing topics like female illiteracy, identity, and societal constraints. Chughtai's Lihaaf (The Quilt), for example, sparked bold discussions about female desire and autonomy in a conservative society, while Hyder's Aag Ka Darya (River of Fire) wove complex tales of history, identity, and womanhood.

Today, contemporary Urdu women writers from both India and abroad continue this legacy, tackling evolving issues with an emphasis on intersectionality, questioning patriarchy, and exploring the multidimensional identities of women. The conference helped the women writers to assess feminist writing. It further paved the way for new voices and themes, ensuring that feminist Urdu literature remains vibrant and reflective of contemporary issues.

Ref.: siasat.com

***

Rashid Jahan: The Bad Girl Of Urdu Literature
Vaishnavi Mahurkar

Educated in Lucknow and New Delhi, Rashid Jahan was the first woman to write about the plight of the women with courage and forthrightness. She is an iconoclastic writer, associated with the Progressive Writers' Movement, who dared to challenge oppressive societal structures. She goes by many names, like – the spark that lit the fire, the rebel with a cause, radical and controversial Urdu feminist of 20th century, and the bad girl of Urdu literature.

Jahan was born in 1905 in Aligarh, to Sheikh Abdullah and his wife Begum Wahid Jahan. Her father, who established the Women's College in Aligarh Muslim University, was the leading pioneer of women's education in India. She was trained as a gynaecologist but is better known for her transparent, raw, ideologically oriented works of fiction she produced after becoming one of the founding members of the Progressive Writers' Association. Ismat Chughtai's work was highly inspired by Rashid Jahan – the only member from the left-wing oriented progressive writers' movement.

"She spoilt me because she was very bold and used to speak all sorts of things openly and loudly, and I just wanted to copy her," Chughtai would later write.

The Person

Jahan had so many sides to her personality – she was a doctor, a writer who was gravely engrossed in the issues of her times, an avowed communist, and a pioneering activist invested in social change. She was a woman ahead of her times in every respect; and continues to be a source of inspiration for women. Jahan was the personification of the nascent feminism which had begun to take roots in South Asian soil.

Rashid Jahan was one of the foremost feminists of the 20th century – carving out a space for women to talk about issues that deeply shaped their life like religion, science, their bodies and sexuality, and modernity. All this created a new or alternative discourse about the women's issues at the onset of modernity. She inherited this legacy from her father who was invested in several movements on reform and education. Her father founded a widely circulated Urdu journal by the name Khatun (Woman) in which her mother was a consistent contributor. With the influence of both her parents, it was evident that her leanings towards writing about the social and political situation were deeply rooted in her upbringing and the influence of the left ideology which furthered her on this path.

Jahan was one of the quartet that published a compendium of short stories called Angarey, published in 1932, which was followed by the storm of controversies making Rashid Jahan known as Angarewali in the vernacular space. She officially joined the Communist Party in 1933. She simultaneously became a symbol of emancipated women in progressive families and that of a brat, a bad girl in others.

The Writer

Rashid Jahan's bold writings were not to create scandal but to incite people to think and reflect about the times they were living in. She worked towards reforms necessary in domestic and social life. She boldly attacked the social set-up, patriarchy and Muslim culture through her writings; bringing in deeper questions of body, sexuality, public spaces, and women.

One of her most acclaimed short stories is "Dilli Ki Sair" (A Visit To Delhi) – an exceptional yet simple account of how women cannot occupy public spaces, and how the male gaze penetrates even through the confines of the burqa. The story questions male privilege in a simple and clear narration. Here is an excerpt which is emblematic of her direct style of tackling such sensitive issues

"Well, we sat in the train from here and reached Delhi. There 'he' met some wretched station master acquaintance of his. Leaving me near the luggage, 'he' vanished. And I, perched on the luggage, wrapped in a burqa, there I sat. First this damned burqa, then these cursed men. Men are anyway no good but when they see a woman sitting like this they just circle around her. There is no opportunity even to chew paan. One damn fellow coughs, another hurls a remark. And I... breathless with fear. And so hungry... that only God knows. And the Delhi station! Bua, even the Fort would not be as huge. Wherever one looked, one saw nothing but the station, the railway lines, engines, and goods trains. And what scared me the most were those blackened men who live in the engines!"

Angare (Burning Coals), released in 1932

was a compilation of groundbreaking short stories and Jahan's best-remembered work. Rashid Jahan, along with Sajjad Zaheer, who edited it, Ahmed Ali, and Mahammudu Jafar were the young authors of Angare – an anthology of ten short stories which turned controversial. These writers who belonged to the upper strata of the Muslim community paved a way for a new literary space.

Rashid Jahan's work is embedded in feminist concerns of the turbulent times she was witness to, in which the thrust towards radical social justice was gathering more importance than ever. Her motivation to write was a social one, one that ached to bring forth the issues faced by Muslim women into everyday discourse; and to influence the readers to reflect and question the society and begin to transform it in ways they can. She used literature as an instrument of social reform. She wrote extensively for magazines and literary journals which are unfortunately lost to today's reader. But what remains of her short stories and plays is a rich account of oppression in the society, one that I would argue continues to ring true even today.

Her other well-known contribution to Angare was Parde Ke Peeche (Behind the Veil).

In it, the wife's illness and her husband's indifference to it weaves together a narrative condemning patriarchal society and its seclusion of women, and its oppression through the domesticity of the woman. Her work is quite reflective of the gender relations present in the times she lived in. It is a sociological analysis of the spaces women occupy like the zenana (women's quarters) and the skewed gender roles they reflect, with the materiality of the veil being the first barrier to inclusive spaces. She wrote about issues that were hitherto untouched by male or female writers and hence it becomes extremely important to look at the thin yet brilliant corpus she leaves behind.

Being a doctor, Jahan was highly concerned with women's health, their relationship to their bodies, and how they are not really taken care of in the society that constantly sees women as caregivers and nurturers. Her work is often claimed to be a bit rough and unfinished but one has to remember that she wrote not to achieve literary finesse but to create a space to talk about the issues she thought mattered.

Her work and life can be said to personify the following Toni Morrison quote "If there is a book that you want to read, but it hasn't been written yet, you must be the one to write it." She wrote about things she thought weren't being written about and needed ample attention.

Though the corpus of her work is slender and her life brief, she left a mark through her literary output which was illustrative of the world enclosed and oppressive, of the Muslim women in her times; which still continues to ring true in contemporary times. This so-called 'Bad Girl' of Urdu Literature made an exceptional contribution towards building the South Asian women's movement and towards modern literature.

Ref.: feminisminindia.com

***

Feminism in Urdu Literature
Lalit Gupta

Dr Mushtaq Ahmed Wani's latest book in Urdu 'Feminism in Urdu Literature', being first of its kind comprehensive account about feminist writing in Urdu literature by a writer from Jammu and Kashmir, is undoubtedly a significant scholarly work.

Dr Mushtaq Ahmed Wani, who hails from village Behota, Marmat, Doda, and having 25 years experience as teacher in School Education Department, is well known writer of short stories, scholar and critic. His Ph.D. thesis later published as a book was titled 'Takseem Ke Baad Urdu Novel Mein Tehzeebi Bohran'. His other publications in Urdu include two anthologies of short stories; 'Hazaron Gum' and 'Meetha Zehar' and two works on Research and criticism; 'Aina Dar Aina' and "Etibar-o-Mayar'.

The present book-an abridged version of the mammoth thesis submitted by the author to Rohil Khand University, U.P., for the successful award of Doctor of Literature (D. Lit) degree-is an encyclopedic work which while tracing the socio-cultural status of women in major ancient civilizations also takes into account the 19th and 20th century women rights movements in America and Europe that led to the unprecedented freedom of expression and action enjoyed by the fairer sex in the modern times.

Today, the Feminist consciousness emerging as a spirit of the age has emerged as a global trend. It has now become a movement or school-of-thought popular among the writers of modern sensibility. The whole movement of feminism, feminist theory and criticism has been the rediscovery of a hidden tradition of women's writing and the rediscovery and republication of a number of novels and other works by women.

Like other parts of the world, educated women in the sub-continent are also fully aware of their rights and the problems faced by them. Urdu literature is becoming richer by women's writings and enjoys a certain amount of freedom of expression in this segregated society. The history of women's writing in Urdu literature is not a recent phenomenon. But unfortunately, the male politics as present in Urdu circles kept this view suppressed for a long time and only recently there is an effort to highlight the writings of feminist writers.

Feminist writing in fiction writing can be traced in modern Urdu fiction and Ismat Chughtai is the first feminist fiction writer in Urdu. Other important fiction writers include Quratulain Haider, Khalida Husain, Fatima Hassan, Gillani Bano, Bano Qudsia, Zahida Hina, Mumtaz Shireen, Jameela Hashmi and Azra Abbas and many more. They have enriched Urdu literature with their writings. The name of Quratulain Haider is not comparable with other writers. She is one of the greatest novelists in Urdu and her novel 'Aag Ka Dariya' is a masterpiece of fiction writing. She has written her novel in the technique of stream of consciousness, such as Virginia Wolfe and James Joyce. She has also written short stories such as 'Sita Haran', 'Jila Watan' and an autobiographical novel, 'Gardish-i-Rang-i-Chaman', a cultural historical document about changes in history and culture. Dr Mushtaq Ahmed Wani's book is divided into seven major chapters. The first chapter traces the rise of feminist socio-cultural movements in America, Great Britain and Germany along with situation of women in Indian society. The second chapter deals with feminism and world literature as well as traces development of women writing in Urdu in India by enumerating names and their works.

The third chapter is about a brief survey of feminist tendencies in pre-Independence Urdu women poets. While the fourth chapter highlights feminism in poetry of post-Independence female poets with special reference to poems and gazals starting from Ada Jafri to Frida Rehmat Allaha. The fifth chapter deals with feminism in Urdu novels of Deputy Nazir Ahmed, Rattan Nath Sharshar, Mirza Mohammad Haji Ruswa, Rashada Al Khiri, Prem Chand, Krishan Chander, Rajinder Singh Bedi, Nazar Sajjad Haider, Razia Sajjad Zaheer, Ismat Chugtai, Jamila Hashmi, Bano Qadisa, Razia Fiaz Ahmed, Jeelani Bano, Wajida Tabussum, Farida Rehmat Allah and others.

The sixth chapter takes into account the feminist elements in Urdu short stories starting with Nazar Sajjad Haider and followed by Mumtaz Shireen, Rasheed Jahan, Ismat Chugtai, Quratulain Haider, Ameena Abu-al-Hasan, Bashri Rehman, Zakia Mashehadi, Wajida Tabussam, Asha Prabhat, Qamar Jahan, Nigar Azim, Tarunam Riyaz, Qamar Jamali, Shakeela Rafiq,

Sultana Mehar, Nagma Zia-ul-Din, Zahida Hina, Nazma Usmani, Kehkashan Parveen, Kehkashan Anjum, Farida Rehmat Ullah, Renu Behl, Sayeeda Nighat Farooq and others. The seventh chapter contains conclusion followed by bibliography.

Dr Mushtaq Ahmed Wani's present book by presenting a broad survey of Feminism in Urdu Literature has thus emerged as important scholarly resource for scholars as well as lovers of Urdu. Other than providing an overview of feminism in Urdu literature, the book would be especially beneficial to the large number of students of Urdu literature in Universities, colleges and schools of the State as a ready reference for the study of general history and development of literature in Urdu as well.

Ref.: dailyexcelsior.com

***

Feminism, social reform and Rashid-ul-Khairi
Rauf Parekh

CONTRARY to what is commonly believed, feminism in Urdu literature is not something new. The first traces of feminist views in Urdu can be found as early as in the sixth and seventh decades of the 19th century, as reflected in the writings of Nazeer Ahmed Dehlvi (1830-1912) and Altaf Hussain Hali (1837-1914).

Though not feminist in the strict sense of the word, these writers were concerned about the status of women in the subcontinent's society. With their reformist thoughts and moralistic views, Nazeer Ahmed's novels sound too didactic but he had realised the lack of proper educational facilities for the women in his society and the disastrous consequences. The absence of proper textbooks for girl students prompted him to write some books in the shape of novels with which he began teaching his own children. On the other hand, in Hali's poetry one finds some poems that advocate the rights of women and raising their status in the subcontinent's society. Before Hali, a woman was depicted in Urdu poetry mostly as sweetheart, but Hali reminded that she can be a mother, sister and daughter, too.

It was, perhaps, Rasheed Jahan who can truly be called Urdu's first feminist writer and whose feminist views were echoed in the writings of scores of women writers later on, such as Ismat Chughtai, who followed the path. Also, Mirza Azeem Baig Chughtai was one of the earliest writers of Urdu whose views can be termed as feminism. But that was not before the first quarter of the 20th century had passed. And it was Moulvi Mumtaz Ali (1860-1935) who took the real significant step by launching an Urdu magazine Tehzeeb-i-Niswan from Lahore in 1898, exclusively for women. The Aligarh-educated Mumtaz Ali had launched this magazine against the advice of Sir Syed Ahmed Khan (1817-1898) who was not in favour of sending girls to schools or even establishing girls' schools. Not only did Mumtaz Ali launch the magazine but made his wife, Mohammadi Begum (1878-1908), its editor. She is the first woman to have ever edited an Urdu magazine.

The last decade of the 19th century was a

revolutionary one for women's education in the subcontinent for it saw an acceptance for the idea of women's education from Aligarh Movement in 1899. After Sir Syed, his son Syed Mahmood and Justice Ameer Ali had convinced Muhammadan Educational Conference for adoption of a motion favouring female education.

This unleashed an era of reformist trend and a kind of 'reformist feminism' in the subcontinent as well as in Urdu literature. Although most of the proponents of female education and reforming the societal attitude towards women's status for their uplift were men, they were, however, not true feminists as they neither fully believed in the equality of the sexes nor did they advocate women's rights the way modern feminists do today. But these voices were genuinely perturbed by the manner in which women were treated and the way women themselves behaved.

One of the most prominent figures who launched a campaign for women's rights and their education in the latter half of the 19th and early 20th century was Rashid-ul-Khairi. He blended reformist and didactic teachings with literary works and is considered among the pioneers of

Urdu short story along with Munshi Premchand and Sajjad Hyder Yildirim. A novelist, short-story writer, essayist, historian, humorist, poet, translator and journalist, Khairi in his literary works, which he penned in quite a large number, portrayed the lack of education and manners in middle-class Muslim women and its ill effects.

Born Mohammad Abdur Rashid in January 1868 in Delhi, Allama Rashid-ul-Khairi wrote over 90 books and booklets. Ismat, a magazine launched by him in June 1908 from Delhi was exclusively published for women. The magazine stood for women's education and was soon acknowledged as a supporter of rights of women. Other periodicals that Rashid-ul-Khairi launched for women include Tamaddun, Sahaili, Banaat and Jauher-i-Niswan.

Rashid-ul-Khairi belonged to a noble and literary family. From his ancestors to the present day, many generations of this family have rendered valuable services for the promotion of Urdu language and literature. Abdul Jabbar Khairi and Abdus Sattar Khairi, the famous political and religious activists, too, came from the same family. Dr Dawood Usmani's book Allama Rashid-ul-Khairi aur un ke khandan ki adabi khidmaat ka tanqeedi jaeza successfully captures the essence of the literary works of this eminent family. It is in fact Usmani's doctoral dissertation and he has done real hard work to analyse different aspects of Rashid-ul-Khairi's life and his works. Published by Anjuman Taraqqi-i-Urdu Pakistan, the 528-page book is divided into 10 chapters. Aside from Rashid-u-Khairi's life and works, the book also takes into account the literary works by the descendants of Rashid-ul-Khairi, which include Raziq-ul-Khairi, Khatoon Akram, Amina Nazli, Sadiq-ul-Khairi, Saad Khairi, Haziq-ul-Khairi, Raziqa Khairi, Saima Khairi, Safoora Khairi, Zaira Khairi and Hina Khairi.

A rich bibliography and an index have added to the value of the work.

Rashid-ul-Khairi died on February 3, 1936, in Delhi.

Ref.: dawn.com

***

The 'F' factor in Urdu Literature
Shazia Tasneem

Dr Nuzhat Abbasi is one of Pakistan's best-known contemporary women poet, who also has a most natural prowess and elegance with which she brings verse to life. A poet as well as a social curator and critic, she also explores feminism and relishes the contradictions and complexities around her in her verses. Whatever she has penned is a result of the urge from within herself to write on that subject. Dr Abbasi heads the department of Urdu literature at a private university. With four published books, alongside contributions to various magazines and other publications, this progressive poet is an important presence on the map of Pakistani poetry in Urdu. She is associated with good number of literary guilds and the president of Dabistan e-Ghazal. She also has participated in International Urdu conferences and Mushairas. A frequent face in literary activities, Dr Abbasi received Parveen Shakir Aks-e-Khushboo award for her book of poem 'Waqt ki Dastak'. She is widely acclaimed for her sharp and incisive poetic expression, for having a feminist view, and for celebrating women's voice and attitude in the universal human struggle for equality, justice, and freedom. Dr Abbasi is a poet who has carved a niche of her own. She has achieved a place in Urdu literature, where she is the supremo of soft feminine diction, melting voice and a tone that many would long for. When it comes to analysing literary works of Dr Abbasi, it turned out to be more prolific than most of her contemporaries. She has authored two collections of poems, a book of literary criticism and research titled Nuskhaha-i-Fikr. Prior to publishing these books she had published her PhD thesis 'Urdu ke Afsanvi Adab me Nisai Lubo Lehja' (feminine tone and accent in Urdu fiction writing). Her book explores the history of feminism in Urdu fiction writing.

Early female writers in Urdu did not write by their own names and went by suffixes like 'daughter of', 'wife of' or 'mother of', hiding behind a man's identity, living as his shadow like Zahida Khatoon Shervania who penned as ZKS with a hidden identity. But the scenario changed with time and women rejected this kind of identity that was dependent on a man. They came forward and started writing with their real names. The very first hint of feminism that we see in Urdu literature is when women gave up their titles of 'Mrs' and 'Daughter of' and the like and made their own identity in the world of literature back in the early 1900s. In an interview with The Express Tribune, Dr Abbasi defines grey lines of oppression and inequality in society while mapping the perceptivity of feminism—the 'F' factor in Urdu literature.

STF: How would you define feminism and its presence in Urdu literature?

NA: The concept of feminism is clearly defined as a movement for women's socio-economic and political rights. It is a philosophy of life and way of thinking. Feminism is also a practical activism. This concept took a sharp rise during 20th century in both East and the West. It is a school of thought and its influence can be seen on every walk of life and every field of life. It is evident in arts, sociology, politics, and literature too. We have been watching wide ranging gender discrimination from centuries on. The basic theme of feminism is to eliminate gender discrimination and achieving equal status for women. One should not consider it as a movement against men.

STF: Did really female writers and poets play a role in shaping up the 'F' factor in Urdu literature?

NA: Of course, they play a leading role in constructing feminism in Urdu literature. In fact, they inspired the present generation too. Feminism and literature co-exist from the very first day the movement was born. It was an awakening being recorded in words by female creators of words. No doubt that the forerunners of this women's movement were female writers. It is the reason that we can clearly see the influence of feminist school of thought and the feminist value in literature and prominence of woman like Virginia Woolf. Like literature in other parts of the globe, we can find the influence of feminism in Urdu literature too and not anyway it is borrowed from the West. In an undivided, greater Indian subcontinent women were largely involved in science and fine arts even thousands years ago during Vedic period.

STF: How this 'F' factor has been influencing Urdu poetry?

NA: In Urdu literature women have been contributing their feminist skill and sensitivity to poetry, fiction, novel, drama, humor, travelogue, analytic and other creative writings. With the movement spreading its wings, women found poetry as a ready podium to express their thoughts, voice their concerns and to claim their biological rights. If we talk about influence of feminism in Urdu poetry, we have a list of women poetesses who not only collected their inner emotions and feelings to paint their thoughts and to highlight the issues that they confronted. At least they were being heard and read. Their protests were being lodged against discrimination and their messages were being conveyed to the curators of segregated society. These poetesses created masterpiece of literature. We have an array of names of female poetesses who received stunning success in their creative pursuit starting from Mah Laqa bai Chanda, Zaibunnisa Makhfi, Zahida Khatoon Shervania ZKS and Lutfunnisa Imtiaz to Ada Jaffery, Kishwar Nahid, Perveen Shakir, Fahmida Riaz and Shahida Hassan.

STF: How will you evaluate the power of feminist consciousness in contemporary Urdu poetry?

NA: There is a new approach developed in Urdu feminist writing. The contemporary Urdu poetesses are creating feminist literature that is based on their personal and collective issues. They have evolved a unique poetic tone. These poetesses created fine technique of symmetry, diction, style, and phraseology. They are creating rich written words, in some cases better than their predecessors as modern writers and poetesses enjoy many facilities and resources that their predecessors really did not have. They have thus been able to reach a large audience of women and articulate an explicitly feminist narrative so powerful that compel us to revisit the spirit of contemporary feminist poetry again and again.

STF: How feminism has become a popular movement or school-of-thought among modern writers?

NA: Women's participation and joining in Urdu literature has smartened the statement of language. The feminine notes and tones are very rich in terms of usage of words, presentation, and style. Their works are powerful enough to hold a larger audience. There was a time when women were not allowed to talk, participate in discussion and writing their thoughts. It was considered as taboo. But women creators were powerhouse of skill and used superfine word arrangement with layers of their thought. Their spirit and skills have been transpired to the poets and writers of new age.

STF: Do you think Urdu literature is becoming richer by women's writings?

NA: In all over the world, women have contributed a unique thought, voice, tone and mood to the field of literature. Women have expressed their thoughts and imaginary that has enriched the literature. Let us talk about Pakistan. Here too women writers/poets are fully aware of the issues in the society. They are raising socio-economic issues. They are a bold voice of equality and rights for women. During the last century women of Urdu literature became more significant and creative. Today's women are educated and empowered too. They have creativity of highest order and not less than men in any way, if compared. Urdu literature is no exception. There is a dire need to do research of feminism in Urdu literature to understand its importance and worth, not to segregate it by labeling as womanly literature. The aim of feminism in Urdu literature is to express women's own thoughts in own way, own style, language and inborn creativity and to display their approach towards life. Women writers/poets are creating characters that they see around them. They weave in words what they experience as women and animate those in words. Definitely, they have a role in enriching Urdu literature.

STF: When feminist elements enter into Urdu short stories?

NA: With feminist literature there emerged the concept of Gynocriticism to construct a female framework for the analysis of women's literature. Women creators have comprehensively contributed to fiction too. They have produced extremely valuable contents while experimenting with their very precise identity and being. Feminist elements in Urdu fiction writing can be traced in Urdu short stories starting with Nazar Sajjad Haider and followed by Mumtaz Shireen, Rasheed Jahan, Ismat Chugtai, Quratulain Haider. Other important fiction writers include Quratulain Haider, Khalida Husain, Fatima Hassan, Gillani Bano, Banu Qudsia, Zahida Hina, Jameela Hashmi and Azra Abbas and many more. They have enriched Urdu literature with their writings.

STF: Whom you would like to credit for introducing feminist element to Urdu literature?

NA: My research topic was feminist voice

and tone in fiction writing and the thesis was published in 2013. It is a deep topic. In my opinion feminist element is noticeable in all category of Urdu literature including myth or dastan, fiction, poetry, and novel. In the early 20th century there was a significant development in writing of novel and fiction in Urdu literature. Women writers had started producing novel and fiction equally with men. They used their inner strength and talent. They used their own thoughts and diction, poured down all their feminine sensitivity and emotion on the flowing words that were impossible for men authors. Prominent among those women writers were Rashidatunnisa, Mohammadi Begum, Nazar Sajjad Haider, Khursheed Jahan, Momtaza Shireen, Asnat Chugtai, Qurratul Ain Haider and Jhadija Mastur. Jameeka Hashmi,Hajra Masrurm Jilani Banu, Banu Qudsia and of course how can I forget Nurul Hooda Shah.

Ref.: tribune.com.pk

***

Translating 'Feminism' in Urdu
Sheema Kermani

I was extremely excited when I heard that a book on feminism and feminist studies has finally been published in Urdu. Since the last five years, the word 'feminism' has very much become part of the everyday conversation and dialogue in Pakistan. This is basically because of the much-discussed, much-talked-about and much-criticised event known as 'Aurat March', which was initiated by a group of feminists in Karachi in 2018.

However, when I held the book in my hands and read the title — Aurat, Justujoo Aur Nisai Andaaz-i-Fikr [Woman, Struggle and the Female Style of Thinking] — I was, to be honest, taken aback. Was the book going to be about feminism, or about femininity? How does the word 'feminism' translate into the Urdu language? Will the book be able to explain feminist ideology to the reader and how the two concepts and ideas differ?

Even though many women — especially

young women — are coming towards feminist ideas, not many are clear about what feminism actually stands for. There is much false propaganda against feminism and this is reinforced by fundamentalist groups and certain elements of the media that see women's liberation and emancipation as a threat.

There is not enough awareness about feminism in Pakistan; the little that people do know about it is very biased and seen from the lens of a patriarchal society, therefore it is very essential and creditable that a book on feminism in Urdu is now available. This makes this book very welcome and one must congratulate the publishers, the printer and the editor. Readers owe a great debt to the book's publishers — the Centre of Excellence for Women's Studies (CEWS) at the University of Karachi (UoK) and the Anjuman Tarraqqee-i-Niswan — and Karachi Studies Society, which has served as consultant. It is wonderful that they have deemed it fit to publish a book in Urdu on feminism.

From the point of view of the contents, the book is interesting. Nasreen Aslam Shah, head of the department at CEWS, has compiled 10 papers written by herself, her faculty and her former students. There is much to inform readers about the history of the women's movement in these essays.

A compilation of essays on feminism in Urdu is a welcome development, but could have been better thought through

There is no doubt that critical assumptions, historical circumstances and ideologies generally have been hostile towards women's movements and there are not enough works to read about women's contribution towards the development of societies. Shah's book is an attempt to make available for Urdu-language readers a group of works that together bring various thoughts and approaches to feminist ideology and create a narrative on patriarchy and its contested margins.

The debates, on what constitutes 'women's work' and what are women's roles, have had to change over the years. As feminists, we do need to question words such as "izzat" [honour] and "zyadti" [excess] when it is used for the English word 'rape'. Detailed feminist scholarship will offer new interpretations, new words, new vocabulary, new narratives, new norms and practices.

These are the kind of questions that must be

raised in books on feminism. The women's texts in this book document the many-faceted and often-challenged arguments within the women's movement as crucial to an understanding of the feminist movement and the resistances it encounters and engenders.

In the preface, written by Shah, we are informed that, in 1989, Women's Studies Centres were set up in five public universities of Pakistan, in the cities of Karachi, Lahore, Islamabad, Quetta and Peshawar. The library of the CEWS at the UoK holds many books on women's studies, but since almost all of these are in English, it became imperative that a book on feminism in Urdu should be considered. Thus, the present volume emerged.

During the reading of the preface, the Urdu word "hawala" [reference] occurs repeatedly and I was dismayed to find that it has been used at least 15 times in the three-and-half pages of the preface. It is certainly not a word of literary value, and the constant repetition smacks of poor proofreading.

March 8 is the International Women's Day and it gets mentioned as a rallying point for activities on women's issues, but its significance, history or background is not explained. Since the book has been written keeping students and academic scholarship in mind, one feels more consideration should have been given to explaining how and why this particular day is celebrated around the world.

The first paper is by Dr Seema Manzoor, assistant professor at CEWS, UoK, and titled 'Nisai Tehreek Ki Taareef-o-Adabi Tajziya' [History of the Women's Movement and Literary Analysis]. She chooses to begin with what I consider a cliché couplet by Allama Muhammad Iqbal:

"Vajood-i-zan se hai tasveer-i-kainaat main rang

Issi ke saaz se hai zindagi ka soaz-i-daroon"

I would roughly translate this into English as: The image that this world presents derives its colours from woman/ She is the lyre that imparts pathos and warmth to the human heart.

One can question how appropriate this couplet is to begin a book on feminism. One would argue that the concept of woman as decorative goes against the very basis of feminism. Surely, the attributes of womanhood are more than softness, sweetness and love. However, Manzoor does give references and quotes from early feminists such as Mary Wollstonecraft as well as contemporary feminists such as Judith Evans. She argues that feminism helps women develop self-confidence, assert their independence and end discrimination. She concludes that, for women to become self-reliant and independent, it is essential that all subjects need to be rectified and gender and class discrimination must end; only then can an equal society be formed.

Dua Rehma, lecturer at CEWS, writes on the different phases of the women's movement internationally and the 'four waves' of feminism. It is an informative essay and gives the reader data and names of international feminists who struggled as suffragettes for the vote, Black women who fought against slavery, the equal rights movements, Simone de Beauvoir, Betty Friedan and Germaine Greer. There is also mention of the #MeToo movement.

Dr Shagufta Nasreen, assistant professor at CEWS, takes on a slightly more analytical approach as the title of her paper itself conveys — 'Nisaiyat: Makaatib-i-Fikr' [Feminism: Schools of

Thought] — and describes the different approaches towards feminism as well as explaining the differing ideologies of liberal feminists, Marxist feminists and radical feminists.

An attempt to explain the difference between sex and gender and how to resolve this confusion is taken up in the essay by teaching associate Dr Shazia Sharafat. This is followed by assistant professor Dr Asma Manzoor's paper on the history of the women's movement in the Subcontinent. Other contributors include teaching associates Dr Shagufta Jahangir and Dr Rukhsana Siddiqui and assistant professor Dr Alia Ali. In the final essay, Shah concludes with the need and importance of feminism and for feminist research with a holistic approach.

A problematic aspect of the book is that it seems the papers have simply been compiled, rather than planned as a collection, and this leads to a lot of repetition of the same material or information, which is irksome.

I was also saddened to find that the Aurat March — a turning point and one of the most important landmarks for the women's movement in Pakistan — is not mentioned in any of the papers, even though the book was published in

May 2021, while the Aurat March began in Karachi in 2018. This event has shaken up the very structures of patriarchy in Pakistan and brought issues of the women's movement into mainstream public debate, redefining sexual mores in a changing contemporary society.

In patriarchal ideology throughout the years, women have been depicted as stereotyped — they have not been accepted as researchers and it has mostly been men who have undertaken research studies. Male sexism has judged and decided women's roles as researchers or writers. Therefore, a 'feminist culture' has not been allowed to develop. Tasks have to be assigned, themes located, areas of debate defined and feminist criticism and ideology has to be authoritatively established.

Once we have a better understanding of feminism, we can develop a theoretical and political critique of our patriarchal society, unpack the oppression of women and ensure their full citizenship in society.

Although there are far too many typing errors and proofreading faults running throughout the book — a sad situation, because one certainly expects a level of quality from a university publication — one hopes Aurat, Justujoo Aur Nisai Andaaz-i-Fikr will be the seed for further books on feminism in Urdu in the near future, so that feminist scholarship in Pakistan can develop further into an institution of humanistic discipline.

Ref.: dawn.com

***

Fragments from the body torn: Fahmida Riaz's fearless legacy
Aleezeh Fatima

"Amma, why do we associate women with love and heartbreak?" my 13-year-old self asked my mother, the reason I know my language.

"Because they're very soft, and they know how to love," she replied, braiding my hair for school. I had more questions, but she hurried us all to school before I could ask them.

But the question never left my mind. Whenever we talk about revolution, independence, politics, communism—anything that alters society—it is associated with men. All the "meaningful" art, the kind that has the potential to change society and people, is linked to male artists, while female poets are often sidelined, their work reduced to themes of love and heartbreak.

Personally, I don't see love as a problem—I believe in it. My issue is with the limitation placed on women's work. And so, at 13, I began searching for feminist writers. I did not fail.

Hence, this International Women's Day, I bring you the first episode of Poetry Beyond Romance, where you embark on a journey to explore poetry through my lens.

To begin with, I completely agree with my mother—women do know how to love, and they are very soft. Which is why, no matter what theme they choose for their art, they create magic. My first lesson of ambition, hope, resistance and resilience was Fahmida Riaz, whose poem 'Kuch Log Tumhe Samjhayengey' is my guide to life.

Defiance, poetry, and unyielding courage:

Riaz, one of the pioneers of feminist thought in Urdu poetry, was born on July 28, 1946, into a literary family from Meerut, British India. Her father, Riaz-ud-Din Ahmed, an educationist dedicated to shaping Sindh's modern education system, passed away when she was only four. In the years that followed, it was her mother who raised her, nurturing within her a love for literature.

From a young age, Fahmida immersed herself in Urdu and Sindhi poetry, later mastering Persian—an influence that would shape her poetic expression. She took her first steps into the literary world as a newscaster for Radio Pakistan, her voice carrying words that would one day shake the foundations of tradition.

Despite her fiery intellect, society still demanded that she conform. After graduating from college, she was persuaded into an arranged marriage and spent years in the United Kingdom with her first husband, working with BBC Urdu and earning a degree in filmmaking.

But life had other plans. After a divorce, she returned to Pakistan, reclaiming her independence with her young daughter in tow. In her second marriage to Zafar Ali Ujan, a leftist political worker, she found not just companionship but a shared ideological fire. Together, they raised two children while navigating political resistance and personal trials.

Riaz's poetry was never just about love—it was about defiance, survival, and the unbreakable spirit of a woman who refused to be silenced. Her personal struggles—of loss, displacement, love, and rebellion—were etched into every verse she wrote. She spoke not just of heartbreak but of revolution, not just of desire but of freedom. In a world that sought to confine women to soft whispers, her poetry roared.

Her poem *'Kuch Log Tumhain Samjhayengey'*, particularly my favorite verses, truly embodies the fighter's spirit she had.

※

کچھ لوگ تمہیں سمجھائیں گے
وہ تم کو خوف دلائیں گے

※

جو ہے وہ بھی کھو سکتا ہے
اس راہ میں رہزن ہیں اتنے

※

کچھ اور یہاں ہو سکتا ہے
کچھ اور تو اکثر ہوتا ہے

※

پر تم جس لمحے میں زندہ ہو
یہ لمحہ تم سے زندہ ہے

※

یہ وقت نہیں پھر آئے گا
تم اپنی کرنی کر گزرو

※

جو ہو گا دیکھا جائے گا

The Urdu word 'Rahzan,' roughly translated as 'thief,' implies that when a woman decides to pursue something, she must endure countless obstacles—whether in the form of people or intangible barriers. Women are bound by so many chains that hold them back when making decisions.

But this poem? It embodies hope, resilience, and a 'woman-to-woman' message—an unwavering reminder to never give up on your dreams, no matter how difficult the path may seem.

And the best part? I'm going to take you on a journey through her life—after which, this poem will make even more sense.

A rebel in verse

Before Riaz became a name etched in history, she was a woman who defied the boundaries imposed on her—both in life and in poetry. She worked in an advertising agency in Karachi before daring to launch Awaz, her own Urdu publication.

But in General Zia-ul-Haq's Pakistan, where fear was law and silence was survival,

Awaz became a target. Its bold, politically charged content made the state uneasy. As punishment, Riaz and her husband, Ujan, were charged with multiple offenses. Awaz was silenced. Ujan was imprisoned.

Yet, silence was never an option for Riaz. She believed that art must remain sincere and uncompromising. "There is something sacred about art that cannot take violation," she once said. "One should read extensively to polish expressions. I read Platts' Urdu-Hindi to the English Dictionary like a book of poems. I love words." Words—her chosen weapon, her unwavering rebellion.

But the system had declared war on her. More than ten criminal charges were filed against her under Zia's dictatorship, including sedition under Section 124A of the Pakistan Penal Code. The state wanted to erase her voice, but an admirer of her work bailed her out before she could be imprisoned. With her sister and two small children, she fled to India under the pretense of attending a mushaira. It was there that Amrita Pritam, her friend and a literary giant in her own right, reached out to Prime Minister Indira Gandhi to secure asylum for her. In exile,

Riaz found solace in Delhi, teaching at Jamia Millia Islamia, where she also learned to read Hindi.

But exile is never just a physical displacement—it is the ache of being torn from your soil, the longing to return. For seven years, she lived away from home, her children attending school in India, her husband eventually joining them after his release from jail. Then, as history shifted, Zia-ul-Haq's death paved the way for her return. She came back to Pakistan on the eve of Benazir Bhutto's wedding reception, stepping onto her homeland once again—welcomed not just by friends and admirers but by the echoes of the battles she had fought.

Yet, the war against her hadn't begun in exile. It had started years earlier, when she first dared to write. When she first dared to speak.

Zia emerged on the political scene, brandishing a version of Muslim nationalism the likes of which the country had never witnessed. In 1979, the Hudood Ordinances were enacted—laws designed to discipline women into submission, forcing them into narrowly defined ideas of morality and obedience. But Fahmida had never fit into the spaces drawn for women, and she wasn't about to start now.

She was thirty-two then. Just five years earlier, she had published Badan Dareeda (Torn Body), a collection of poetry that shattered the silence around female desire, autonomy, and agency. And all hell had broken loose.

To men, Badan Dareeda was obscene, an attack on the so-called values of "Muslim culture"—whatever that meant to those who dictated it. But to Fahmida, it was simply her truth.

She had written it in London, where she found herself trapped in an unhappy marriage, one that had been arranged shortly after her graduation from the University of Sindh. At the time, she did not think of herself as politically conscious. She had settled into life and marriage with the quiet resignation of a passenger taking an empty seat on a moving train. But poetry has a way of awakening even the quietest of souls.

And once she had found her voice, she refused to give it up.

Poetry as resistance

Riaz's poetry was never confined to love, romance, and heartbreak—the themes often imposed upon women poets. Her words tore through the fabric of oppression, speaking of politics, feminism, freedom, and the human condition. For her, feminism was not just an abstract ideal but a lived reality.

"Feminism has so many interpretations. What it means for me is simply that women, like men, are complete human beings with limitless possibilities. They have to achieve social equality, much like the Dalits or the Black Americans," she declared.

"The discrimination is very obvious, very subtle, very cruel, and always inhuman." She demanded a woman's right to walk freely, to write without being branded immoral, to exist without fear.

Decades later, as intolerance grew in India, she stood once more with her poetry as her resistance. On March 8, 2014, she recited Tum bilkul hum jaisey nikley (تم بالکل ہم جیسے نکلے) at the Hum Gunahgaar Auratein (ہم گنہگار عورتیں) seminar. The poem, a mirror held up to both nations, compared the rise of Hindutva in India with the rise of Islamic fundamentalism in Pakistan.

*

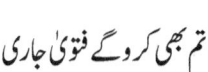

ہو گا کٹھن یہاں بھی جینا

*

دانتوں آ جائے گا پسینا
جیسی تیسی کٹا کرے گی

*

یہاں بھی سب کی سانس گھٹے گی
بھاڑ میں جائے شکشا و کشا

*

اب جاہل پن کے گن گانا
آگے گڑھا ہے یہ مت دیکھو

*

واپس لاؤ گیا زمانہ

Safe to say, many of the brave decisions I've made in my life—including becoming a journalist in a country riddled with censorship, where I am often unable to say what I truly want—stem from Riaz's poetry. She refused to bow to decaying norms and held her head high.

She was the true embodiment of how women, when they escape confined cages, can achieve wonders and bring about the change the world once told them they couldn't. 'Women will conquer the world, and they'll do it with all the sensitivity and love they contain,' my 25-year-old self recently told my mother.

Ref.: tribune.com.pk

***

The future is feminist literature and it's called Behenchara Magazine
Khadija Muzaffar

Twenty-three-year-old Misha Ali Farhana has an unusual last name. Most people take their father's name as their surnames. Others go for the slightly confusing hyphenated situation that will only get more confusing down the line. But when you're destined to start a feminist literary magazine, it's only fitting that you carry your mother's name at the end of your own.

This is exactly what Misha does when she writes 'Farhana' — her mother's name — at the end of her name, instead of Nauman (her father's name).

The credit for this rebellious move doesn't really go to Misha, however, as it dates all the way back to when she was in utero, and devoid of any preferences, feminist or otherwise. Her parents, however, were not devoid of any such inclinations.

When Nauman — a radiologist — and Farhana — an English teacher — got married, they decided that they would split all household duties 50/50. If Farhana had to go to work, Nauman would pick up all the chores, and vice versa. When Farhana got pregnant, Nauman was determined to give the child his wife's name as the surname, regardless of gender.

"Even before I got married, I knew that if I ever had a child, I would want the mother's name to be attached to it, even if it's a boy. Mothers are the ones who put in the hard work and actually struggle," he told me over Zoom one day, joined by his wife, from their house in Lahore.

Both of their families disapproved of the idea, so much so that on the day Misha was born, Nauman's father was caught whispering in the hospital orderly's ear to include his son's name on Misha's birth certificate — an act which Nauman did not permit.

Misha is very cognisant of the role her parents played in her feminist upbringing. She says she's lucky to have parents who are staunch feminists and never really made her feel like she couldn't do something just because she was a girl. "My parents actually call themselves feminists, and they're quite blunt about it too," Misha said.

Growing up in a household where

womanhood and equality were valued and honoured seemed to add to the anger she felt at the world, which did not always value those things the same way.

The idea

During her time at Formanite Christian College, where she is currently a senior, Misha joined a women-only listening circle hosted by two of her peers, where members talked about that weeks' topic. As she heard about all the atrocities being committed against women and minorities, she realised that people her age wanted to express their anger, fear and hurt through their words and their art, and that there wasn't really a space where they could safely do that.

Sure, secret support groups for women like Soul Sisters were popping up on Facebook daily, and there was Aurat March, the annual political demonstration held in cities all over Pakistan on International Women's Day but none of these places served as a concrete platform that would be easily accessible to everybody.

Misha envisioned a neutral online space that could be taken in any direction: an archive of thoughts, ideas and opinions, a database of important resources, a place to host events and talks and discussions, and perhaps most importantly, a safe space to host people's contributions, in whatever shape they took. Then she met Alina, and things took shape, fast.

The chance encounter and execution

Alina Anjum was a junior at FC College when she first met Misha, who was then in her freshman year. According to her, their story started with a chance encounter and an offhand remark that turned into a sisterhood.

Having spotted each other at university, they found out they were interested in the same things, passionate about the same causes and enjoyed being angry at the world together. And to truly drive in the fact that it really was Fate that brought them together, they discovered they lived only one street down from each other.

Misha, who had by now decided that the safe online space she was envisioning would be a feminist magazine, knew in her head that Alina was the best person to do this with.

Alina had been a longtime volunteer at the Aurat March, was a member of the Tehreek-e-Niswan, a woman's organisation in Pakistan, and ran her own organisation that supported survivors of sexual harassment and abuse called 'Chadar'. She was fairly well-known in feminist circles, and Misha knew that people would trust her.

Their idea for the magazine was to have people send in their contributions. Everything from poetry to artwork to book reviews was welcome. Misha and Alina would then sift through the submissions to filter out any purposefully spiteful content because as they told me, they like to post every submission they get.

"Apart from correcting typos, we don't even fix grammar. Because it's your written expression, we don't want to change the way you've written it," Alina said. "Also, it's your goddamn colonisers' language, it doesn't have to be perfect at all. If you want to write in broken English or broken Urdu, write it! We'll publish it."

The only time they feel obliged to censor anything is when it's homophobic, transphobic, or just generally defies the principles of intersectional feminism. In March 2020, they published the first digital issue of Behenchara Magazine, an online literary feminist publication that is now five issues strong and has almost 2,000 followers on Instagram.

Behenchara, sisterhood and the act of

rebellion

Behenchara means sisterhood but interestingly, the word doesn't really exist in Urdu. The actual word that behenchara stems from, is bhaichara, which means brotherhood and unity (bhai is the Urdu word for brother; behen means sister). In a way, just the act of coining the term behenchara is an act of feminist rebellion: I believe in the Sisterhood and I believe it deserves a word of its own, thank you very much. It's not too different from the kind of questioning that turns a chairman into a chairperson, or mankind in to humankind. Just one more attempt at inclusivity and representation in a seemingly never-ending chain of such attempts.

The choice of name was a good one. It serves as a blunt explanation of what the magazine stands for. Still, Misha is taking no chances. She doesn't want there to be any confusion, which is why the 'About Us' section of the magazine's website is actually a PSA announcing that the crux of the magazine may not need too much explaining. 'If it must be stated, then we stand for feminism, minorities and all victims of unnecessary discrimination, but primarily, feminism/womxn.'

The hefty PSA goes on to declare that Behenchara is an independently run magazine that doesn't allow for any interference. It is for this reason that Misha and Alina are the only ones on the Behenchara team; they have a distinct voice of their own and adding other people to the mix would dilute it. The end result is complete autonomy over what goes out.

The PSA also mentions that they 'neither seek nor shun controversy', which is part of why Behenchara has managed to escape from the kind of onslaught that is typical of any forum where feminism is the topic being discussed, front and center.

Feminism can be a hard topic for people to talk about anywhere in the world. In Pakistan, complications arise, as they almost always do, when religion is brought into the mix. But strangely, Behenchara has been able to evade any and all sorts of criticism, which is highly unusual for a forum discussing women's rights, a topic which everyone seems to have an opinion on.

The underdogs

One reason for this is that Behenchara hasn't blown up and become a household name yet like other media entertainment websites have. It's unlikely that they will attain that kind of attention because their entire ethos and mode of operation is so different. Behenchara is more of a social venture in an e-magazine's clothing. They try very hard to stay as far away from being commercial.

"I don't think [Behenchara] can get that mainstream success because mainstream channels would probably not want to come to us. We don't allow for advertisements on our website," said Misha, adding "If it ever does get this sort of fame, though, then yeah, definitely. We'd definitely get a lot of backlash. That should be expected."

Alina has another theory. She believes the way Behenchara is packaged saves them from the ire of the internet. The fun colours, the doodles, the informal witty language scattered throughout their Instagram posts and their website all seem to signal to people that this is not a serious publication, and hence isn't deserving of their hate or anger.

The contributors and content

Their latest issue is called 'Violence, Bodies and Shame' and was intended to allow women to decompress and share their anxieties and concerns after the news of a particularly horrific sexual assault case shook the country.

"We've got the contributions for it, but it's packaged in the traditional Behenchara way, which is like there's a doodle on it and there's a specific way to write on it and we have our own quirky spin on it," Alina explained. "That kind of makes people think that it's not serious, which means when trolls want to engage, they just don't. But people still find it relevant, they contribute, and they still talk to us and share their stuff."

To me, it seems like the real appeal of Behenchara lies not in the publication's quirks or how non-commercial it is but rather because of how palatable and inoffensive the content and its language is. As a literary magazine, the focus is more on creative pieces and personal essays rather than hard-hitting heavily opinionated pieces that are rich in discourse and academic jargon.

There's never an air of passive-aggressiveness, or blind rage, and the website gives people no reason to feel intimidated or defensive. This happens organically, according to Misha, who insists that it is not a deliberate move on their part.

"I don't want to sound vain, but we are very kind to our contributors, and we're very welcoming, so even they don't feel any sort of tension. Obviously, there are certain things that can trigger and anger and enrage, but when they know that there is this sort of calm welcoming fireplace-lit sort of place to sit down and just talk, they're not very enraged."

The funding, or lack thereof

Irtifa Nasir believes that Misha is being modest about her own role in the positive reception of Behenchara. Irtifa was one of Misha's professors at university in Lahore and is the only benefactor the magazine has had so far. Earlier this year, she donated Rs10,000 to the magazine so that Misha and Alina could pay for a new website. She thinks the reason that Behenchara can connect to people so easily is because Misha herself has that ability.

"I see the way she markets it on social media, the way she writes, the posts, doodles, everything and because it's Misha's signature style, it's her personality, she projects it onto Behenchara," Irtifa told me. "Obviously with somebody who's so genuine and so raw and real, it's hard to not like such people, right?" She thinks the awkward, self-effacing but witty style of Behenchara's Instagram posts help to not intimidate people, which can be a huge thing when you're talking about a topic as serious as feminism.

So far, the magazine is on the right track. They've had a steady stream of at least nine contributions each issue, sometimes even more. They run an advice column, where the mysterious and anonymous 'Aapa' (older sister) dishes out advice on topics ranging from boyfriends and husbands to unyielding parents. They host interviews with celebrities and industry experts. Things are going well. But still, Misha feels like there is a lot yet to be figured out.

For starters, they aren't paying contributors yet, which both women feel very strongly about. "We feel even worse that we can't pay the people who make cover art for us because, God bless them, they do it for free, and they do it voluntarily," she said. But in order to start paying people, they're going to need money, which might prove to be difficult because they don't want to turn Behenchara into something that makes money.

The future

So then, what does the future look like for a feminist literary magazine in Pakistan?

A lot of applications for grants, and a lot of unpleasant words about capitalism. "Now every time we make a decision, it's like, wait, what about 10 years from now, will we have the funds for this? Okay, so if we apply for a grant, how long will it last?" Alina said grimly. But beyond grants and the financial realities of the real world, Behenchara has big plans.

Misha wants to someday expand to an actual print publication, maybe one with lower quality paper, but hey, at least you can hold it in your hands, right? They're thinking about starting a podcast sometime next year. Till that happens though, Misha will be working hard to keep Behenchara going with its current model, one inoffensive doodle at a time.

Ref.: dawn.com

***

Fahmida Riaz: The act of translation as mourning
Asad Alvi

In an earlier essay for Images, Fahmida Riaz: the woman who decolonised feminism, I paid tribute to the legacy of the late Urdu feminist poet, who left us last year in November.

In that essay, I touched upon Fahmida's engagement with concepts such as the nation, body, home, belonging, culture and the work of translation.

In this follow-up piece, which has resulted out of a renewed interest in her work, I want to build upon an injunction introduced in the first essay — "the best form of mourning a writer is to read their body of work" — and include the act of translation.

Translation acquires a new meaning in this manner for me: of mourning the life of the Other by inhabiting her text, internalising the vision of this text through the act of translation, as though it were my own vision, and rewriting this vision into the language I best know, the English language. To make the vision yours; to transform the dead into the living.

It is essential, therefore, that this rewriting of visions does not turn the dead into a static thing, does not take advantage of the fact that the dead can not communicate with us. When this happens, translation becomes violence, and the rewriting, narcissistic: one can recreate Fahmida in any manner one wants, and in doing so, destroy the vision.

For example, Fahmida's poetry relies on a heavy use of intertextuality and allusion to mythologies: words such as karb, jalal, jamal and maqtal haunt her work. Yet karb is not anguish, because karb is also a wordplay on Karbala: sound mimetic of meaning.

And jamal and jalal cannot be translated as majesty and strength, because they are meant to be read together, and in translation they lose their rhythm.

Fahmida, while she was using them, had felt that rhythm inside her body. For me to access the vision, I have to ensure that these rhythms are kept intact in my own body. Otherwise the vision will be lost. Therefore, in my translation of the following texts, I have let these words remain.

I begin by translating the preface to A Body Torn/Badan Dareeda, which is appearing here in its first ever translation.

Badan Dareeda was Fahmida's first collection of explicitly feminist verse. The poems were about sex, religion, womanhood, pregnancy, menstruation, spirituality and desire.

They were written in an extraordinary burst of creativity during 1969 and 1974, and upon their publication in 1975, received a series of harsh criticisms, including being labelled as "pornographic."

For Fahmida, therefore, the form of the preface serves a special political function: to respond to these accusations and to assume the role of the literary critic.

Today, the preface to Badan Dareeda is a cornerstone para-text for understanding the inception of feminist literary criticism in Urdu literature.

It also serves as a cultural history of Urdu literature during the Zia era, and a history from below of the kind of censure and oppression that women experienced during that period for their work.

As memorable as Audre Lorde's Poetry is

Not a Luxury and Gloria Anzaldúa's A Letter to Third World Women, the letter is nothing short of a Manifesto for Third World women and queer peoples struggling with violent histories of patriarchy.

The translated preface culminates in the translation of five poems from the collection, which has become a hallmark of feminist expression in the Urdu language.

I invite you to meet Fahmida with me, in the liminal act of translation, beyond the wall that divides the living from the dead.

~~~~~

The Preface to A Body Torn/Badan Dareeda by Fahmida Riaz
Translated by: Asad Alvi

Drag this body torn of mine through the town
for my self belongs to them: to the earth, and the living

~ Ghalib

My first collection of poetry was published in 1967. The name of the collection was: Pathar ki Zaban. Tongue of Stone. Then, in between 1967 and 1972, I wrote many more poems. They have been collected and are appearing here for the first time in this collection, Badan Dareeda. A Body Torn. These 50 poems are the labourious work of seven long years. You will find them very different from my previous work.

Which is why there are those in this city who are not happy with it. They think the collection is fahash, or pornographic. Then there are those who think that the poems have been deliberately produced to create shock value. These observations have led me to ask an important question: why does a poet write? Let us mull over this question for a bit. Some might say that a poet writes for amusement. Others might say that she writes for fame. The assumption here is that a poet writes for self-interest. Never have there been greater lies.

If, at all, a poet takes an interest in herself, it is because she discovers there the movement of all history: its violence, its paradoxes, its terrible weight. The poet is not alone in feeling this weight. In our modern age, because human life has been commoditised, every citizen feels a karb rising inside themselves: a sense of displacement, an alienation. The citizen attempts to resolve this feeling. Some experience a return to religion. Others seek a sense of the sacred within their own professions.

Think of a kumhar, for example, who comprehends the meaning of the entire cosmos in the rotation of a potter's wheel. Or the doctor, who roams around frenzied searching for a cure to an important disease. Or the lawyer, who finds in the value codings of the law and its multiple iterations some notion of divine justice. Human beings are driven for a desire to transcend the limitations of their self and aspire to something greater. We do not necessarily blame them for these ventures.

But we seem to take an issue with the figure of the intellectual. Poets, artists and philosophers are not altogether different in their desires for something greater than any other person. If there is one thing that perhaps separates them from these others, it is that they desire the intuition of this transcendence in extremis.

This means that the poet, more so than any of these other people, has to let go of her self-interest. She has to efface her own self in order to transform herself into the figure of the dissenter. Those too locked in their own identities, those who have never produced a single sound of dissent, cannot possibly know how much exhaustion comes with such a transformation. It cannot be done from a vantage point of self-interest or narcissism, as is the accusation against me. This transformation is jigar-kharash. It ruptures the body of the one doing it. In between the silent existence of trauma within one's body and actually transforming this silence into language upon one's lips, a lot is to be lost.

It is easy for those who are conjuncturally outside the space of this transformation to denounce it. They will never know the pain of it all. Yes, it is true that the identity of poets is celebrated. Long after the poet has transformed the silence which has been circling inside her body like rings of fire into language, she is hailed into recognition. There is in this period an element of sar-khushi, or self-affirmation in her life. Everyone wants to comprehend her in the complete manifestation of her jalal and her jamal. And yet, one casually forgets the subtext of violence that has led to the making of this jalal: the karb that she has had to endure.

It is the transformation of this karb into language that gives birth to poetry. In the attempt of this transformation, the poet more often than not loses her own head. And there are those poets who came before me. Which poet, indeed, in the workshop of existence, has not faced the hour when she has had to stand before the maqtal and lose her head? Which one of them has not had to pay for her language, her utterance, sometimes with her own life?

If, indeed, I am forced to stand before this maqtal today and face the gallows, I should face them with my head held high. My poems are the trace of a mangled head: emanating sounds even as it is suspended from ropes. In the light of this, A Body Torn has taken the form of a razmia, or the sound of rupture. And if such rupture indeed shocks a people, then consider the poet as having achieved her purpose: she has managed to disturb them.

Ref.: dawn.com

***

'Mera Jism Meri Marzi': Revisiting Sahir Ludhianvi's Ode To Women

Raza Naeem

The legendary progressive poet Sahir Ludhianvi (1921-1980) was born 99 years ago today in Ludhiana, in what is now Indian Punjab. I have dealt with elsewhere why his circumstances and upbringing made him into a feminist even before he became a communist and progressive writer, but he has given Urdu literature four or five very powerful feminist poems (whether he is talking about women or about his concept of love). We can detect traces of his feminism in one of his earliest poems Taj Mahal, which is about how there is a class element to love; the love between working-class lovers can never be equated with that between two privileged members of society, which is based on their class interests. Thus, the monument of Taj Mahal actually becomes a symbol, not of beauty, but of a fake form of love.

Then he has given us the two poems denouncing prostitution, namely "Aurat ne janam diya mardon ko; mardon ne use bazaar diya" (Woman gave birth to Man; and Men gave her the marketplace) and "Chakle" (Brothels). There is also his poem "Nur Jahan ke Mazar Par" (At the Tomb of Nur Jahan) which posits the dead queen as the "daughter of the people" and connects it to his wider denunciation of patriarchy.

Given that today also marks International Women's Day, and several Aurat Azadi Marches are taking place across the country, it is fitting that we also commemorate Ludhianvi by revisiting a poem which was not part of the poetry published in his lifetime; but became part of his unpublished poetry collection which was eventually published after his untimely death. Titled simply as "Aurat" (Woman), but more frequently anthologised as "Log Aurat ko Faqat Jism Samajh Lete Hen" (People Judge a Woman Merely to be a Body), it takes issue with something that is one of the centrepieces of the Aurat March in Pakistan this year, and has been severely roiling many patriarchs in Pakistan in the lead-up to March 8th – 'Mera Jism Meri Marzi' (My Body My Choice). Ludhianvi discusses the contradiction that whatever a woman does, a man's ultimate criteria of judging her will be her gender and her body, not her spirit. This patriarchal attitude is not new but centuries old, persisting across time, space and culture. So much so that the woman is forced to be in a 'no man's land' between life and death. Towards the end of the poem, Ludhianvi wonders aloud whether this attitude towards women is bound to persist even with the advent of modernity but, unlike many propagandist poets, he does not pontificate on a solution, which adds to the beauty and allure of the poem. Those marching for the rights of women today in Pakistan are well-primed and well-equipped to take this challenge forward in a satisfying manner. This poem is presented here in an original English translation both as a way of celebrating the feminist and communist poet that was Sahir Ludhianvi, but also as a different, albeit poetic, way to understand that the beauty of a woman ultimately lies in her spirit.

Woman
By: Sahir Ludhianvi

*

"People judge a woman merely to be a body!

That she does possess a spirit too is lost on

everybody.

*

What the spirit is, they plainly fail to understand
For them the body's demand is their every command
The spirit dies leaving the body to be a walking corpse
That they neither understand nor recognise this reality is beyond remorse.

*

For how many centuries this habit of fear has continued
For how many centuries this custom of sins has endured
People judged every scream of the woman as a song
Whether it be the time of tribes or the practice of the city throng.

*

The generations continue by force, bodies meet at the point of the sword
This happens among us, but not among the un-knowing birds
We the carriers of civilisation among the human brood

Would that there be anyone more barbaric in this neck of the wood?

*

An extinguished spirit lying within a body's structure

I think at which place should I let my fate rupture

I am not alive in that I seek death to support my plight

Neither am I dead in that the sorrows of life take flight.

*

Who will tell me, who should I ask

Till when life be set in the groove of wrath, it's quite a task

Till when the conscience of time not open its eye

That an end to this rule of cruelty and tyranny be well-nigh?"

Ref.: tribune.com.pk

***

www.ingramcontent.com/pod-product-compliance
Lightning Source LLC
LaVergne TN
LVHW010408070526
838199LV00065B/5918